E.W. Miles
Middle School Library
501 Route 110
Amityville, N.Y. 11701

THE CHOCOLATE WAR

by
Robert Cormier

Teacher Guide

Written by
Gloria Levine, M.A.

Note

The text used to prepare this guide was the Laurel Leaf softcover published by Dell. The page references may differ in other editions.

Please note: Please assess the appropriateness of this book for the age level and maturity of your students prior to reading and discussing it with your class.

ISBN 1-56137-206-4

Copyright infringement is a violation of Federal Law.

© 2000, 2004 by Novel Units, Inc., Bulverde, Texas. All rights reserved. No part of this publication may be reproduced, translated, stored in a retrieval system, or transmitted in any form or by any means (electronic, mechanical, photocopying, recording, or otherwise) without prior written permission from Novel Units, Inc.

Photocopying of student worksheets by a classroom teacher at a non-profit school who has purchased this publication for his/her own class is permissible. Reproduction of any part of this publication for an entire school or for a school system, by for-profit institutions and tutoring centers, or for commercial sale is strictly prohibited.

Novel Units is a registered trademark of Novel Units, Inc.

Printed in the United States of America.

To order, contact your local school supply store, or—

Novel Units, Inc.
P.O. Box 433
Bulverde, TX 78163-0433

Web site: www.educyberstor.com

Table of Contents

Plot Summary 3

Background on the Novelist 4

Initiating Activities 5
    Anticipation Guide, Viewing, Log, Verbal Scales,
    Brainstorming, Role Play, Prereading Discussion and/or
    Writing Questions

Chapter-by-Chapter
    Chapters Contain: Vocabulary Words
    and Activities, Discussion Questions and
    Activities, Predictions
    Chapters 1-4 7
    Chapters 5-8 9
    Chapters 9-13 11
    Chapters 14-16 13
    Chapters 17-20 15
    Chapters 21-24 16
    Chapters 25-28 17
    Chapters 29-33 19
    Chapters 34-36 20
    Chapters 37-39 22

Post-reading Extension Activities 24
    Post-reading Discussion Questions, Suggested
    Further Reading, Writing, Essay Topics, Listening/
    Speaking, Debate, Drama, Language Study, Art,
    Music, Research

Evaluation: Rubric for Essay-Writing 29

Assessment 30

Plot Summary

The novel's central character, Jerry Renault, is a student at Trinity, a private high school run by Catholic priests. Jerry's mother died a short time before the opening of the story; communication with his hard-working father, a pharmacist, is minimal. Jerry's chief escape is on the football field, and he is anxious to make the freshman team.

When the ambitious, sadistic Brother Leon takes charge of the annual fund-raiser—a chocolate sale—he enlists the support of the Vigils, a secret society of students that the brothers neither officially recognize nor disband. Archie, the "Assigner" who is the brains behind the Vigils, despises Brother Leon but delights in making students squirm as much as Brother Leon does. Archie agrees to see that the boys sell twice as many chocolates as usual, at twice the usual price, and later learns why Brother Leon is so anxious for success: Without authorization, Brother Leon has already spent $20,000 of school money on the chocolates.

Meanwhile, Archie summons Jerry's friend "Goober" to give him one of the Vigils' notorious "assignments." (As with every assignment, Archie must first draw a marble from a box; if he draws the sole black marble—which has never happened—he must carry out the assignment himself.) Goober is horrified when Archie orders him to loosen the screws in all the furniture in Brother Eugene's classroom, but like most of the Trinity students, Goober is afraid to refuse a Vigil assignment. Later, the class dissolves in predictable chaos as the furniture falls apart, and Brother Eugene disappears after reportedly suffering a nervous breakdown.

Next, Archie gives Jerry an assignment: Antagonize Brother Leon by refusing to sell chocolates for two weeks. Each day tension mounts as Brother Leon calls each name for the sales count, and each day Jerry dares to answer "no." The eleventh day arrives and for some reason even Jerry doesn't quite understand, Jerry continues to refuse to sell chocolates. Others congratulate him for showing guts, and general sales slacken off, which angers Archie and Brother Leon.

Archie meanwhile manages to humiliate an entire class by arranging a prank and then tipping off the teacher. Every time Brother Jacques says the word "environment," the boys in his class leap up and perform a jig. The teacher uses the word repeatedly, exhausting the boys. Archie's rival, Obie, recognizes Archie's duplicity and his hatred for Archie intensifies. Obie demands that Archie do something about Jerry's defiance and is annoyed when Archie merely orders Jerry to sell the candy. Heartened by Jerry's refusal to conform, Frankie Rollo refuses an assignment. This time, however, Obie's supporter, Carter, defies Archie—who eschews physical violence—by giving Rollo a beating, to the delight of the other members.

Jerry becomes the victim of several anonymous attacks: his favorite poster is vandalized, he is struck viciously from behind during football practice, his landscape watercolor assignment is taken, and he gets harassing phone calls. Chocolate sales rise as public sentiment shifts against Jerry. Upset by his role in Brother Eugene's breakdown, Goober quits the football team and begs Jerry to start selling chocolates before the others break him as they have broken Goober and Brother Eugene.

Archie has had the dangerous Emile Janza more or less under his thumb ever since the day Archie pretended to take an embarrassing picture of Emile Janza masturbating in the men's room. He has told Janza that someday he will give the picture to him in exchange for a favor. When Archie tells Janza to get Jerry, Janza provokes Jerry by calling him a "queer" and then attacks Jerry with the help of several small, vicious boys.

When all the chocolate has been sold, Archie holds a student "assembly" on the athletic field. At Archie's suggestion, Jerry agrees to settle with Janza by having a boxing match. What Jerry doesn't know is that Archie has organized a raffle: Each buyer fills in a description of who is to strike what blow (e.g., "Janza, right to jaw") and the fighters are to comply. The fight proceeds according to the rules until Janza aims a blow at Jerry's groin and Jerry tries to defend himself. The bloodthirsty crowd goes wild and Janza begins pummeling Jerry, who realizes that he has sunk to the level of the animals around him, and then passes out.

Somehow Brother Jacques finds out what is going on and cuts the power to the stadium lights, moments before Obie glimpses Brother Leon, who has been watching the entire spectacle. Goober comforts Jerry, who is taken away in an ambulance. Brother Jacques begins to chastise Archie, but Brother Leon intervenes, praising the boys' "zeal and enthusiasm." To Obie's consternation, Archie has triumphed once again.

Background on the Novelist

Robert Cormier was born in Leominster, Massachusetts, in 1925. The father of three daughters and one son, Cormier said he enjoyed writing about young people because he felt an affinity for them that came in part from having his own children and in part from memories of his own teenage years. "...If I have total recall of anything, it's not facts and figures but the way those years were, and not ever wanting to go through them again. Then when my own children became teenagers, I saw them going through the same things that I'd gone through and realized that they were universal and timeless." (*Contemporary Authors,* New Revision Series, Vol. 23).

The son of a factory worker, Cormier completed one year at Fitchburg State College before landing his first job as a writer for Radio WTAG in Worcester, Massachusetts. Later he moved on to jobs as a newspaper reporter, wire editor, and associate editor of the *Fitchburg Sentinel.* For nine years (1969-78), he authored a human interest column under the pseudonym "John Fitch IV." He became a full-time free-lance writer in 1978, four years after publication of his highly applauded novel, *The Chocolate War.* Based in part on his son Peter's experiences, the novel addresses the pressures of conformity. "Commenting on how he finds the trials that face adolescents both meaningful and inspiring, Cormier states, 'Teenagers...don't have the freedom that adults have...Kids that age want to be independent and free, and they think they are, but they're the most conformist group in the world...' " *The Chocolate War* received numerous awards—including the *New York Times* "Outstanding Book of the Year" award and the ALA's "Best Book for Young Adults." Nevertheless, the novel—like most of his subsequent novels and short stories—is controversial in some circles. His fiction has been criticized for its bleak portrayal of adolescence and has been banned from some school libraries because of its disturbing themes.

Media Adaptations: *The Chocolate War* has been made into a film. Several critics have commented on similarities between *The Chocolate War* and the novel that followed it, *I Am the Cheese,* which has also been made into a motion picture starring Robert Wagner and Hope Lange (and featuring Robert Cormier as Mr. Hertz). *The Chocolate War, I Am the Cheese,* and *After the First Death* were all released as cassettes by Miller Brody in 1982. See the "Further Reading" section at the end of this guide for a list that includes Cormier's other writings.

Initiating Activities

Choose one or more of the following activities to prepare students for the story they are about to read.

Anticipation Guide (See *Novel Units Student Packet,* Activity #1)

Students discuss their opinions of statements which tap themes they will meet in the story. For example:
- It's usually best to go with the crowd.
- These are the best years of my life.
- The Holocaust could not happen today.
- The good guys usually win in the end.

Film

View the video version of *The Chocolate War.*

Log

Have students keep a response log as they read.
- In one type of log, the student assumes the persona of one of the characters (e.g., Jerry). Writing on one side of each piece of paper, the student writes in the first person ("I...") about his reactions to one episode in a chapter. A partner (or the teacher) responds to these writings on the other side of the paper, as if talking to the character.
- In another type of log, the dual entry log, students jot down brief summaries and reactions to each section of the novel they have read. The first entry could be made based on a preview of the novel—a glance at the cover and a flip through the book.

Verbal Scales

After students finish a section of the story, have them chart their feelings and judgments about Jerry using the following scales or others you construct. Students should discuss their ratings, using evidence from the story.

Like	1—2—3—4—5—6	Dislike
Happy	1—2—3—4—5—6	Sad
Mature	1—2—3—4—5—6	Immature
In Control	1—2—3—4—5—6	Helpless
Honest	1—2—3—4—5—6	Dishonest
Fearless	1—2—3—4—5—6	Frightened
Sympathetic	1—2—3—4—5—6	Self-absorbed
Hopeful	1—2—3—4—5—6	Hopeless
Not Angry	1—2—3—4—5—6	Angry

Brainstorming

Have students generate associations with a theme that is central to the story while a student scribe jots ideas around the central word or statement on a large piece of paper. Help students "cluster" the ideas into categories. A sample framework is shown on the next page.

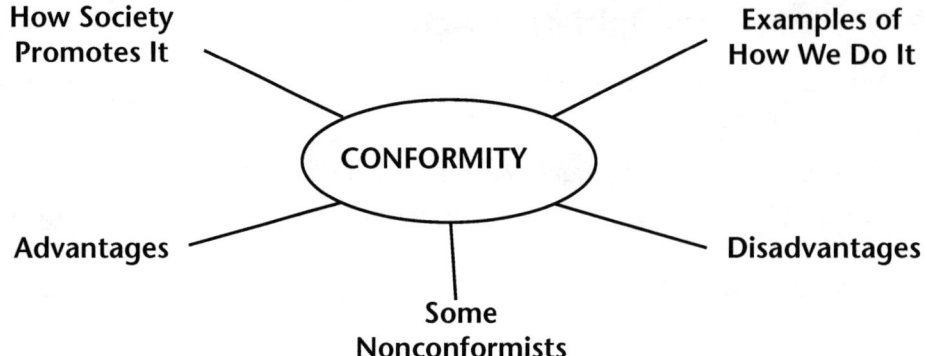

Role Play
Have small groups of students improvise skits demonstrating one of the following situations (analogous to a situation that is central to the story):
- A teacher intimidates his students by singling out individuals for humiliation.
- A group of students intimidates individual students by threatening them physically.
- One student intimidates another by using "psychological torture" or blackmail.
- Young people engage in mob behavior.

Prereading Discussion and/or Writing Questions

Group Decisions and Situations: What are some ways that decisions are reached by a group of people? What is the democratic way? Is this always the best way? Why do we have rules? Is it better to have too many rules or too few? What is conformity? What are its advantages and disadvantages? Have you ever heard of a group that witnessed someone in trouble but did nothing to help? Have you ever been part of such a group? Do people act differently in these situations than they would if they were on their own? How, or why not?

Robert Cormier: Have you ever read any other Robert Cormier stories? If so, what were they like? What did they have in common? Did you enjoy them? What do you know about Cormier and the kinds of things he writes about?

Leadership: What kinds of people become leaders? What are the qualities of a good leader? What skills do you think a good leader needs to have? (Students might come up with a list of skills and abilities, then rank order them.) How is it that criminals and unethical people sometimes become strong leaders?

Violence: What are some of the causes of violent behavior? Why do seemingly "civilized" people sometimes grow violent? How do mobs react to violence? Have you ever been the victim or perpetrator of violence? How did it feel? What is hazing? Why do some college students go in for hazing? Do you think there is anything wrong with it?

Scapegoating: Discuss with the class the notion of "scapegoating"—blaming all the ills of a society upon one person or group. Under what conditions do people look for scapegoats? Who are the individuals or groups that tend to become the victims in these situations? Has anyone in the class ever had a personal experience with "scapegoating"?

Chapter-by-Chapter
Vocabulary, Discussion Questions, and Activities

Chapters 1-4

Vocabulary

grotesque 7	lassitude 8	benevolently 11	languidly 14
surreptitiously 18	contemptuous 20	confrontation 20	ingratiating 23
incapacitated 25	feigning 25		

Vocabulary Activity

Word mapping is an activity that lends itself to any vocabulary list. For words that have no antonyms, students provide a picture or symbol that captures the word meaning.

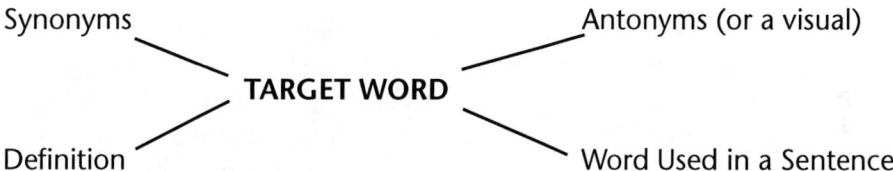

Discussion Questions

1. As the story opens, who has "murdered" whom? What is making Jerry sick? *(Jerry's opponents on the football field have tackled him hard.)* Why do you think he chooses to put himself through all of this? *(He wants to be on the freshman team. Maybe focusing on football—and even on pain—helps him cope with his mother's death.)*

2. What is the connection between what happens in chapter one and what happens in chapter two? How are they connected in time and place? *(Archie and Obie have been observing Jerry on the football field; Archie decides that Jerry is tough and needs an "assignment.")*

3. What are your impressions of Jerry so far? Would he be a friend of yours? (Draw the following attribute web on the board; have students suggest Jerry's characteristics and locate supportive evidence in the text as you jot these down on the board.) *(He acts like a fighter who doesn't give up on the football field; from what Obie and Archie say, we gather that he is 14, the son of a pharmacist. The narrator tells us that Jerry feels guilty when he looks at Playboy. He wears a tie. From the stranger's taunts, we gather that he looks pretty conservative; from his response to the stranger, we infer that he backs off from confrontation.)*

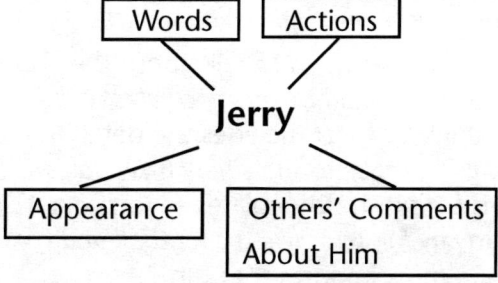

4. What is the coach like? *(He looks like a gangster, curses, spits, yells at his players.)* What do you think of him? Why do you think he is so gruff? Does Jerry mind the coach's attitude? *(He doesn't like to be spat on, but wants the coach's approval.)* Do you think a good coach needs to act that way?

5. Why is Obie annoyed with Archie? *(Obie resents being ordered around by Archie and is angry that Archie is making him late to work.)* Why do you think Archie is holding Obie up? Why doesn't Obie just leave?

6. Why does Obie admire Archie? *(Obie admires Archie's cleverness at coming up with cruel "assignments" and Archie's ability to manipulate people.)* Is Archie someone you would admire? Would you be intimidated by him?

7. Why do you think Archie says that maybe he should "assign someone to the store"? *(Maybe he is trying to control Obie by letting him know he could arrange a prank that might get Obie in trouble at work.)* What sort of assignment do you think he is thinking of?

8. Have students reread the description on page 14: "The shadows of the goal posts sprawled on the field like grotesque crosses." Why do you think Cormier compares the goal posts to crosses on page 14 and again on page 17? *(Maybe Cormier underlining how "un-Christian" the behavior of these boys is, despite their attendance at a parochial school.)* What do you see as you imagine Obie and Archie talking?

9. What do you learn about Jerry's mother? How do you learn this? *(The narrator reveals Jerry's thoughts about how drugged his mother was at the end; Obie reads in his notebook that Jerry's mother died the past spring of cancer.)* What does Archie have to say about her death? *(He is falsely solicitous, then suggests that Jerry needs the "therapy" of an assignment.)* What does that show you about Archie? *(his uncompromising cruelty)*

10. Why does the fellow with the moustache confront Jerry? *(He has noticed Jerry staring at him and his friends.)* What tone of voice do you think he and Jerry use? *(The stranger is belligerent; Jerry is conciliatory.)* Why do you suppose Jerry doesn't just walk away? What do you think the stranger wanted from Jerry? Why does Cormier include the detail that Jerry yanks off his tie once he is on the bus? *(probably to show you that what the stranger has said about Jerry's being "square" has hit home)*

11. What is Archie's opinion of Brother Leon? *(Archie admires Brother Leon's intelligence and ability to be calm under pressure.)* Do you think Archie's thoughts are a reliable source of information about Brother Leon? What does Brother Leon's opinion of Archie seem to be? *(The teacher doesn't seem to like Archie much, but he realizes that Archie wields power among the students.)* How can you tell that neither wants the other to know what is really going on in his mind? *(Brother Leon is nervous, as evidenced by his sweaty upper lip, but he keeps his voice casual; Archie is excited to realize that Brother Leon is nervous, but hopes that his thumping heart doesn't give him away.)*

12. Why has Brother Leon called Archie in to talk about the chocolate sale? *(Brother Leon, who has ordered twice the usual number of chocolates, wants Archie to get the Vigils behind the sale.)* Why do you think Cormier includes the detail that the chocolates are actually Mother's Day chocolates? *(maybe to show how unscrupulous Brother Leon is)* According to Brother Leon, why is selling the chocolates so important? *(Trinity is a private school that needs the money to pay for items like the football and boxing programs.)* Which reasons do you think are most important to him?

Prediction: What do you think Archie's "assignments" are, exactly? How will the Vigils help boost candy sales?

Writing Idea
Rewrite the scene describing what went on in Brother Leon's office. This time tell about the incident from Brother Leon's point of view (with Brother Leon as the narrator).

Literary Analysis: The Lead
An effective opener or "lead" captures the interest of the reader right away, as any good newspaper reporter knows. In various interviews, Cormier has noted that his newspaper work has been helpful in his fiction writing because of the discipline it established and the direct journalistic style it taught him. Have students examine the opener, "They murdered him." How does it capture reader interest? What tone does it set? *(The lead immediately raises a question in the reader's mind. Who murdered whom and why? Once this chilling tone has been set, the reader reads on to find out that the murder is a figurative one. Jerry has been knocked down during a football play.)*

Chapters 5-8

Vocabulary

irrevocable 32	inscrutable 32	nemesis 32	inoffensive 34
sacrilegious 38	wistful 42	accessory 42	

Discussion Questions

1. What "assignment" does Archie give The Goober? *(loosen the screws of everything in Room 19)* Why do you think that assignment upsets The Goober so much? *(He is a good-hearted person who doesn't want to cause trouble and upset the adults who trust him.)* Why doesn't he just refuse to do it? *(peer pressure)*

2. Why was Archie chosen to be "the Assigner"? *(because he is intelligent and imaginative)* What does he like about that role? *(He likes humiliating others.)* What doesn't he like? *(He resents the pressure the others put him under without appreciating what is involved in creating assignments.)* How well do you think Archie understands himself? Why do you think the author mentions Archie's fascination with the Marx Brothers movie? *(He is drawing an analogy between Groucho and himself, two people who create things others don't see the need for.)*

3. How does Archie feel about the Vigils? *(He resents them and feels that he is above them.)* How do the others feel about him? *(They dislike but admire him.)* How does the box of marbles provide "control" over him? *(If he chooses the black marble, he must do his own assignment.)* Whenever he draws a marble, what are the odds that it will be black? *(1 out of 6)*

4. How is Brother Leon like Archie? *(Both like to make people squirm.)* How are their victims—Bailey and The Goober—alike? *(Both are shy, introverted victims.)* Why does Brother Leon enjoy the "games" he plays with students? *(He enjoys abusing his power.)* Have you ever had a teacher like him?

   (Draw the following Venn diagram on the board and have students list likenesses and differences.)

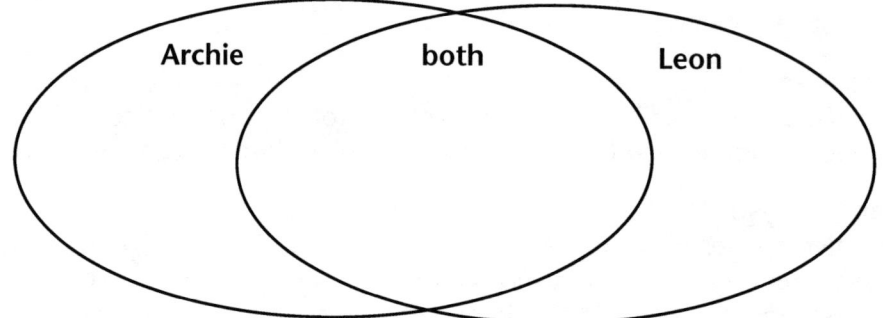

5. How does Brother Leon physically hurt Bailey? *(hits his cheek—"accidentally"—with the pointer)* Do you think it is intentional? Why is it that after the welt appears, "…somehow the tables were turned. It seemed as if Bailey had been at fault all along." Can you think of occasions where people have treated the victim of violence as if he or she were at fault? *(an example: rape victims)*

6. How does Jerry feel about the way Bailey is treated? *(Jerry feels terrible, wishes he were out on the football field.)* Why do you think he laughs along with the others?

7. Why does Brother Leon tell Bailey he "did well"? *(Brother Leon praises Bailey for standing up to his accusations.)* How do you think Bailey feels about that praise? How do you think the other boys feel when Brother Leon turns the tables on them?

8. How do Emile and Archie feel about each other? *(Archie finds Emile amusing; Archie is one of the few people Emile respects.)* What do they have in common? *(Both enjoy tormenting teachers and students.)* Who do you think has the "upper hand"? *(Archie; Emile wants to be like him, a member of the Vigils.)*

9. How well does Emile understand people? *(He knows how to humiliate and unnerve them.)* Why does he wish Carlson had caught him siphoning gas? *(He probably would have enjoyed intimidating him.)* What do you think would have happened? Why do you think he enjoys harassing teachers and students so much? Have you ever known anyone like him?

10. Why does Goober like running so much? *(When he runs he feels free, clear-headed, and graceful.)* Do you feel the same way when you run? Do you have another activity that helps you escape from your everyday world?

11. How is the whole Room 19 experience like a nightmare for Goober? *(He works for hours and gets little accomplished; he worries about disgracing himself.)* What do you think he is most worried about—that he is doing something wrong? that his parents will find out? his teachers? that the Vigils will punish him? Why do others come to help Goober? *(They want to see that the assignment is done completely and the Vigils' reputation preserved.)* Why do you think Cormier describes the first person who comes to help Goober as having the "aspect of the beast"? *(By so describing the boy who is advancing on all fours, the author conveys Goober's sense of a waking nightmare.)* How long is he at the task? *(a total of nine hours)*

Prediction: What will happen when the next class is held in Room 19?

Writing Idea
Respond to the incident between Brother Leon and Bailey by writing a poem. The poem should illustrate the feeling of bitterness, anger, protest, or even hatred that Bailey experienced during that encounter. (These poems are models of "bitterness" poems that you might want to read aloud first: Langston Hughes's "Theme from English B," Calvin Hernton's "The Distant Drum," Theodore Roethke's "Dolor," Matthew Arnold's "Dover Beach.")

Literary Analysis: Irony
Explain that irony is a device involving a contrast between what a situation appears to be and what it actually is. Ask what is ironic about the fact that Brother Leon accuses his students of turning the classroom into a Nazi Germany. *(He, himself, is acting like Hitler by persecuting Bailey and enlisting the support of the group.)*

Conformity Survey
Make an informal survey of the classroom to determine current fads in the way students dress. You will need to tailor the survey to current clothing trends such as brands of sneakers and jeans, styles of shirts and tops, and so forth. You might also include hairstyles in your survey. When tabulation is complete, ask students whether they dress as they do because of their choice or because of peer pressure. What would happen if one person dressed in a completely individualistic manner—for instance, always wore a suit and tie to school? Would the person be accepted, tolerated, or ostracized? Use this discussion to lead into a more serious investigation into peer pressure and how much it affects the lives of teenagers.

Chapters 9-13

Vocabulary
bedlam 57   rangy 61   adulation 64

Discussion Questions
1. How have Jerry and his father handled their grief? *(Except for one moment at the cemetery when they embraced and wept, they haven't shared their grief. Jerry has thrown himself into football. His father's escape is work.)* Is there any way Jerry and his father could have supported each other more?

2. Why does Jerry press his father about whether he ever has wonderful or terrible days? *(He hates to think of how boring his father's life seems, how unexpressive his father is.)* Would Jerry be happier if his father complained more?

3. What is Jerry's father like? *(hard-working, conscientious, uncomplaining, unexpressive)* Why is Jerry bothered by the way his father lives his life? Why doesn't he want to be like his father? *(He hates to think that his life may turn out to be as blah.)* Do you want to be like your parents? Do you think Jerry is being fair to his father?

4. What evidence do you see in this section that both Jerry and his father cover up how they really feel? *[Both say "fine" without elaborating on how they really feel about what is going on in their lives. Jerry starts to talk to his father, then can't figure out what to say without sounding crazy (p. 52).]* What could he say?

5. What do you hear Brother Leon saying as he gives his pep talk about the chocolate sale? *(the importance of school spirit, the need for money to fund various programs, the need to do something for the sick headmaster, successes in past sales)* How do you picture him? *(looking annoyed as the boys hoot at his students trying to put up the posters, which won't adhere to the wall)* How do you picture Archie as he listens? *(perhaps with a contemplative, scheming look)*

6. How do the students in Room 19 react once desks start falling down? *(They rush around pushing everything down.)* How would students react if this happened in your school? Why is Brother Leon so angry? *(He realizes that Archie has engineered this prank, which will take energy and attention away from the sale.)* Do you think anyone feels sorry for Brother Eugene? *(Archie is delighted by his tears; perhaps others feel sympathy, but there is no evidence.)*

7. Why doesn't Jerry mind being called an SOB by the coach? *(It is considered a badge of honor, a sign that the coach accepts you.)* Should Jerry mind?

8. How does the final line of Chapter 12 suddenly turn the mood upside down? *(Jerry is elated about his success on the field; then he finds the chilling summons on his locker.)* What do you picture Jerry doing after he finds the letter on his locker?

9. How does Goober become an underground hero? *(Kids hear about his role in the Room 19 fiasco.)* Does he enjoy that status at all? *(He may enjoy it a little, but he is depressed about Brother Eugene.)* How does Archie continue to intimidate him? *(Archie tries to scare him by telling him not to admit to anything if he is questioned.)*

10. In what tone of voice do you imagine Jerry saying "No" as he refuses to accept the 50 boxes of chocolates? *(quiet, flat)* Why do you think Brother Leon dismisses the class "although the bell had not sounded" (p. 67)? *(He is flustered by Jerry's refusal.)* How do you imagine the students exiting? Does Jerry look at Brother Leon?

Prediction: What will Jerry's reasons for refusing to sell the candy turn out to be? What will the consequences be?

Writing Idea
Imagine that Brother Leon keeps a log on the progress of the chocolate sales campaign. Write three of the entries: one from the day Brother Leon calls the special assembly to announce the sale to the student body, one during the week the sale is postponed, one on the day that Jerry first refuses to sell chocolates.

Literary Analysis: Flashback
Explain that a flashback involves interruption of the action with a scene that occurred earlier. Have students identify a flashback in this section. *(Jerry thinks about the time a few months ago when his mother was dying.)*

Chapters 14-16

Vocabulary

simonizing 69   commiseration 82

Discussion Questions

1. From whose point of view is the opening of chapter 14 told? *(The reader is let in on John Sulkey's thoughts.)* Why do you think Cormier uses phrases like "Let's see" and "of course" in the first paragraph? *(This conversational language signals that these are a character's thoughts.)*

2. What can you tell about John Sulkey and his neighborhood from the descriptions of his customers? *(This sounds like a working class neighborhood; John is responsible, well-liked by his neighbors for whom he cuts the grass, runs errands, etc.)* Which customers can you imagine most vividly?

3. What does John Sulkey like about the chocolate sales? *(John, who is not a good student, enjoys getting awards for high sales.)* How do you suppose the other students feel about Sulkey?

4. What motivates Tubs to sell chocolates? *(He wants to make money to buy his girlfriend a bracelet.)* Why do you suppose his parents don't approve of Rita?

5. How does Paul feel about selling chocolates? *(He doesn't like selling them but enjoys the chance to get out of the house and away from his dull parents.)*

6. What do you learn about the parents of John, Tubs, and Paul? *(John seems close to his parents, who are proud of his sales awards; Tubs' father drinks and his mother drives around to entertain herself, thinks Tubs' girlfriend is too old for him; Paul thinks his parents live useless lives.)*

7. Why has Brian Cochran become the Treasurer of the Chocolate Sale? *(Brother Leon chose him.)* Do you think he enjoys any aspect of that job? *(He hates the job because he is afraid of Brother Leon.)* Would you enjoy such a job?

8. Why is Archie pretending that he has a photograph of Emile Janza? *(He knows that he can use the supposed photo as leverage to get Janza to do what he wants.)* What would Janza do if he found out there is no photo?

9. Why does Janza tell the freshman to get him cigarettes? *(just to intimidate the kid and show off for Archie.)* Do you think the kid will get the cigarettes? What would happen if he didn't?

10. Why do you think Caroni got the F? *(Brother Leon may have deliberately graded his written responses harshly so that he could blackmail Caroni.)* What effect does that grade have on him? *(Caroni is shocked and horrified by the low grade.)* What does it cause him to do? *(He tells Brother Leon about Jerry's "assignment" in hopes that the teacher will raise his grade in return.)*

Cause	Effect/Cause	Effect
low grade	*Caroni shocked/Caroni blabs*	*Leon knows/grade stands for now*

Do you think that Brother Leon will change Caroni's grade?

Prediction: Now that he knows about the assignment, will Brother Leon be able to get Jerry to sell the chocolates?

Writing Idea

Caroni feels terrible after allowing Brother Leon to blackmail him into revealing Jerry's "assignment." Respond to the encounter between Brother Leon and Caroni by writing a confession poem from Caroni's point of view. The poem might begin "Once I." and should explain the "crime" and its consequences. Aim for two eight-line stanzas, but alter this form if you like. You may want to rhyme your lines, but a prose poem is fine.

Literary Analysis: Minor Characters

Minor characters may be introduced for a variety of reasons. Sometimes they are important to the plot. Sometimes they reveal more about key characters. Sometimes they reinforce the theme. Why do you think Cormier introduces the characters of John Sulkey, Tubs Casper, Paul Consalvo?

Literary Analysis: Setting

Ask: What is the novel's setting? (Talk with students about the setting of the story, reminding them that the setting includes the time—approximate year, season—and the place in which the story takes place.) Draw the following graphic on the board and have students fill in the blanks:

Time — (1970s, football season-fall)   Place — (New England private boys' school)

Explain that setting refers not only to the time and place of a story, but to the **social milieu**. Have students look for clues in this section to the social climate in which the boys live. What socioeconomic group are the boys from? What expectations do their parents have for them? How is the time and place in which these boys are growing up shaping their lives? How does the description of the setting reinforce the theme and tone of the story?

Chapters 17-20

Vocabulary

swiveled 89 plummeted 89 claustrophobia 90 vulnerability 92
relief map 95 premeditation 98 pandemonium 99

Discussion Questions

1. Why does Brother Leon look astonished the eleventh time Jerry refuses the chocolates? *(He knows that the assignment is over and expects Jerry to accept the chocolates now.)* Why does it seem "almost as if Jerry and the teacher were reflections in a mirror" (p. 89)? *(Jerry is as surprised by his own actions as Brother Leon is.)*

2. Archie's assignments are acts of cruelty. How is Jerry's assignment cruel? *(By refusing to sell chocolates, Jerry makes Brother Leon anxious about the overall sales; it is also cruel for Jerry to be put on the spot.)*

3. When do you think Jerry decides to continue to refuse to sell the chocolates? *(It seems to be an almost subconscious decision, made at the moment of Brother Leon's inquiry.)* Why do you think Jerry makes this decision? *(Perhaps he wants to prove to himself that he is free to choose.)* In his place, what would you do?

4. How does Jerry feel about the way the others react when he continues to refuse to sell the chocolates? *(He somewhat enjoys their admiration.)* Do you think Goober is wrong to try to get him to sell the candy?

5. Why doesn't Brother Jacques do something about the prank the boys are playing on him? *(He is doing something; Archie has informed him anonymously of the prank so that now he is deliberately using "environment" repeatedly, forcing the exhausted students to jump up each time.)*

6. How does Obie feel about Archie? Why doesn't he tell Archie off? Why does a "small smile play" on Brother Jacques' lips as the students get up five times in fifteen minutes? *(Obie is enraged that Archie made a fool of the class; Brother Jacques is enjoying turning the tables on the students.)*

Prediction: Will Obie get back at Archie for tipping off Brother Jacques?

Writing Idea
The day Jerry's two-week assignment is up, he surprises everyone by continuing to refuse to sell the chocolates. That night he has an awful time trying to get to sleep, and the next morning he wakes up feeling as if he has a hangover. Describe the nightmares he has had during the night. *(Remember that before dropping off to sleep he has been haunted by thoughts of his mother, Bailey, Archie, and Brother Leon.)* Include sights, sounds, smells.

Literary Analysis: Conflict
Conflict, or struggle, drives the plot. There are several types: person against person, person against society, person against nature, and person against self *(inner conflict)*. Have students point out the inner conflict as Jerry struggles with his own feelings in this section. *(Even Jerry is puzzled about why he continues to refuse to sell the chocolates; Jerry has an internal argument with himself on pages 90-91.)* Discuss the other types of conflict present in the story. *(All are present except person against nature.)*

Chapters 21-24

Vocabulary

farce 108	scapegoat 110	calisthenics 111	quota 111
sibilant 113	apathy 113	bellows 115	disembodied 118
precarious 120			

Discussion Questions

1. Why does the author juxtapose the description of Kevin and Danny's conversation with the description of Howie and Richie's conversation? What do they both show? *(Both pairs are talking admiringly about Jerry's refusal to sell chocolates.)* How are Kevin and Howie alike? *(Both would like to stop selling chocolates.)* How are they different? *(Howie is influential, the president of the junior class; whereas Kevin tells a friend confidentially that he would <u>like</u> to quit selling candy, Howie announces that he is quitting.)*

Kevin	Howie
thinks Jerry is right	thinks Jerry is right
jokes about not selling candy	decides not to sell candy
sophomore, wants to be Vigil	President of Junior class

2. Why does Obie have Archie meet him in the gym? *(Obie plans to confront Archie in the sweaty place he knows Archie likes least to be.)* These two don't seem to like each other much. Cite examples of put-downs and provocations during their meeting. *(Archie thinks of Obie as "an obvious stooge, an errand boy." Obie responds sarcastically when Archie responds with "beautiful" to Obie's attempt to light the fire under him about repaying Jerry for his success at defying the Vigils.)*

3. Why doesn't Archie follow through right away on his promise to have the Vigils back the chocolate sale? *(After the assembly, where students hoot, Archie has his doubts about the Vigils' willingness to get involved.)* How does Brother Leon threaten Archie? *(Brother Leon calls Archie on the phone, ordering him to get sales up and convince Jerry to say yes; otherwise the Vigils will be disbanded.)*

4. How is Brother Leon like a "mad scientist" (p. 113)? *(He whispers to Brian in a sinister voice that Renault is the carrier of the "disease." Like a mad scientist intent on his work, Brother Leon has become obsessed with the chocolate sale.)*

5. Why do you think Jerry and Goober have discussed the assignment and the Room 19 incident so little? *(Maybe each is afraid to embarrass the other.)* Shouldn't friends talk about their problems?

6. Why has Goober decided to quit football? *(He feels guilty about his role in the Room 19 incident and doesn't want to give any more to Trinity.)* Is he doing an admirable thing? Is he only hurting himself?

7. Goober says that something "evil" is going on at the school? Do you think "evil" is too strong a word here?

8. What does Archie find out about Brother Leon's involvement with the school's finances? Why do you think Brian Cochran divulged that information? *(Brian mentions that he overheard Brother Jacques arguing with Brother Leon about spending a lot of unauthorized money on the chocolates before the sale began.)*

9. Why does Brother Leon order Archie to get Jerry to say "yes"? *(Brother Leon knows that the other students are beginning to model Jerry; when he agrees to sell chocolates, the others will too.)* What else could he do to get sales up?

10. Why does Brother Leon think that Archie will listen to him? *(Archie knows that Brother Leon has the power to expose the Vigils.)* Why should Archie care whether or not the chocolate sales go down the drain? *(His reputation and that of the Vigils are at stake.)* Who seems to have the upper hand at the end of this section? *(Brother Leon literally has the last word before hanging up.)*

Prediction: Will Archie follow Brother Leon's order or will he find a way to defy him and sabotage the sale further? Do you think Archie is right in his estimate of Obie as being someone who would never have the nerve or know-how to get revenge?

Writing Idea
Goober is very upset. When he tries to explain how he feels to Jerry, he has trouble putting into words the connection between Brother Eugene and Room 19 and not playing football. Suppose that Goober does manage to put down his feelings in his diary that night. Write the diary entry he makes.

Literary Analysis: Resonance
Sometimes an author strings related images throughout a piece of writing to create a particular effect. Ask why Cormier compares the dog that chased Kevin Chartier to "those terrible dogs the Nazis used for hunting down concentration camp prisoners" (p. 102). Have them locate related images in other portions of the novel.

Chapters 25-28

Vocabulary

exultancy 129   sabotaging 134   adversary 134   derision 139
camaraderie 142

Discussion Questions

1. Why does Archie summon Jerry for another assignment? *(Archie is being pressured to make Jerry sell chocolates.)* Are you surprised that the assignment isn't "tougher"? Do you agree with Obie that for once, Archie is "running scared" (p. 126)? Does Archie really think that Jerry will simply begin selling chocolates as assigned?

2. At the meeting in the storage room, why does Archie have various people call out the numbers of boxes they have sold? *(He is trying to use peer pressure on Jerry by showing how much harder the others have been working.)* Why do several boys inflate their numbers? *(Because of peer pressure, they tell Archie what he wants to hear and go along with the crowd.)*

3. How does Archie finally talk to the girl who smiled at him? *(He calls all the Barretts in the phone book and asks for Ellen.)* What does his decision to talk with her have to do with the chocolate sale? *(Having bucked the system by refusing to sell candy, he decides to further break the routine in his life by doing something else he wouldn't ordinarily do.)* Why does that contact destroy "all illusion about her" (p. 129)? *(She has a wise-guy voice and says "crap.")* Is he too idealistic?

4. Are you surprised by what happens to Rollo? *(He refuses an assignment and Carter beats him up.)* Do you think the incident has anything to do with Jerry's refusal to sell chocolates? *(Carter is fed up with Jerry's intransigence and takes it out on Rollo.)* What would you do with Carter if you were the headmaster at Trinity and his role in the incident came to your attention?

5. Why is Archie against physical violence? *(He knows that the school authorities will clamp down on the Vigils if they learn of physical violence.)* Do you think beating up Rollo is worse than using psychological torture—say, embarrassing him in front of the whole school, or getting him in trouble with the teachers?

6. Why does Carter put Archie on "probation"? *(He feels that Archie is being inefficient at getting Jerry to tow the line so that chocolate sales will go up.)* How does Archie plan to get the chocolates sold? *(He will have the Vigils organize the sales and make it "cool" to sell chocolate.)*

7. How is Jerry harassed? *(He gets prank phone calls, someone destroys his poster and sneakers, someone takes his landscape assignment, someone attacks him from behind on the football field.)* What do you think bothers him most? Do you think he regrets his decision not to sell chocolate? Why do you think he feels "ashamed" when he finds the vandalized poster and slashed sneakers (p. 140)?

Prediction: Will Jerry tell his father why they have been getting prank phone calls? Will the pranksters get bored and quit—or will there be other forms of harassment?

Writing Idea
Jerry is being harassed. Someone has attacked him during football practice; someone has taken his landscape assignment; someone has vandalized his locker. Does this remind you of anything that has ever happened to you? Have you ever seen anything like this at your school? Write a brief personal essay about harassment.

Literary Analysis: Suspense
Suspense is a story quality that produces tension in the reader, who is curious about what will happen next. Suspense usually raises one of two types of questions in a reader's mind: What will the outcome be? When will the inevitable outcome happen? Have students discuss how suspense develops in this section. *(The reader wants to know: Will Archie prevail over Jerry? Who is harassing him and what will they do next?)*

Chapters 29-33

Vocabulary

waylaying 144   maverick 156   luminous 159   disheveled 159

Discussion Questions

1. How do the Vigils get sales up? *(They organize teams and go into various neighborhoods; they check in with individuals to see how their sales are.)* How does the reader find out about their methods? *(Brian reflects on what he has seen and heard.)*

2. Why isn't Brian comfortable with the way credit is distributed? *(He knows that some people who didn't sell chocolates are being credited.)* Why do you think the Vigils do this? *(to exert peer pressure; to make it look as if "everyone is selling them")* Is there anything wrong with it?

3. How can you tell that Brian likes being applauded when he makes the entries (p. 146)? *(He realizes that he feels like a football hero.)* Why do you think Cormier decided to compare him to a football hero? *(Perhaps this is a deliberate echo of Jerry's sport, to emphasize that very different people all like to be heroes—to have others' approval.)*

4. When does the general feeling start to turn against Jerry? Why do the others start to resent Jerry? *(Once the Vigils get behind the sale, the other boys drop their live-and-let-live attitude—beginning with the roll call at which Darcy demands to know why Jerry isn't selling chocolates.)*

5. Cite evidence that the Goober feels badly for his friend—but fails to stick up for him. Should he? *(The Goober decides not to sell chocolates in support of Jerry—but doesn't say anything when he is credited with chocolate sales.)*

6. How does Jerry get into a fight with Emile Janza? *(Janza taunts him, calling him gay.)* Could the fight have been avoided? Why do you suppose Emile gets the other attackers involved? Couldn't he "handle" Jerry by himself? Does this scene remind you of anything you have read or seen in a movie—or anything that's happened to you?

7. Why doesn't Jerry want anyone to see him after the attack? Why does he keep his collar up "like a criminal" (p. 156)? *(He feels guilty—as if he somehow is to blame for what happened.)*

8. Why do you think the voices taunting Jerry from below are compared to ghosts, "like someone calling from the grave"? (p. 158) *(This death imagery helps create a chilling atmosphere, conveys how "haunted" Jerry feels—and how deadly are the intentions of his harassers. There is also a parallel with Jerry's thoughts of his mother.)*

9. How much does Jerry's father know about the Vigils' harassment of his son? *(He knows only that someone is making prank calls. Jerry has told him nothing about the Vigils.)* Should he be more aware of what's going on?

10. Why does Jerry consider the fact that his father has taken the phone off the hook, "defeat"? *(He is modifying his behavior rather than confronting the "attackers.")* What else could he do?

Prediction: What will Archie have Emile do next?

Writing Idea: Memory Writing

Think about the encounter between Emile Janza and Jerry. Write down all the sights, sounds, and smells you associate with that scene. Include images that are provided by the text as well as any that came from your own imagination. (What was Emile wearing? What did Jerry hear as the attackers emerged from the bushes? What did he smell as he tried to curl himself up on the ground?) Then write a description of the memories that flood into Jerry's mind when he regains consciousness after the attack.

Literary Analysis: Cliffhanger

Explain that a cliffhanger is a device whereby the reader is left "hanging" at the end of a section, eager to read on and find out how the situation is resolved. Have students identify one cliffhanger in this portion of the novel. (p. 155: Jerry falls into unconsciousness and the reader asks himself—Will he be all right? What will happen to him?)

Chapters 34-36

Vocabulary

desecrated 163	tabulation 165	rancid 165
sanctimoniously 166	cajoling 170	desecration 172
submissiveness 174		

Discussion Questions

1. How do you know that Emile was acting under Archie's guidance? *(Emile berates Janza for having botched the plan by using the small kids—"Janza, can't you do anything right?"—p. 161)* How much of the attack was Archie's idea? *(Emile compliments Archie by telling him how well his idea for using the "queer pitch" worked out. Archie played a large part in the plan to attack Jerry.)*

2. Why does Jerry suddenly feel like a ghost (p. 163)? *(People are ignoring him at school.)* The narrator comments that it was "as if he were the carrier of a disease" (p. 163). Where have you heard that phrase in this novel before? *(Brother Leon described Jerry that way to Brian.)* Do you think the students are acting under orders? Do you think it is Jerry's imagination that the teachers are ignoring him, too? Does this invisibility remind you of the experience of any other character you may have met in literature or film?

3. How does Jerry feel about his momentary "absence of identity"? *(At first he enjoys being left alone.)* Why do you think Jerry's locker has been cleaned out? *(This action further harasses Jerry by conveying the idea that, "It never happened...you don't exist.")* Have you ever enjoyed such an absence of identity? How does Jerry know when he isn't "invisible" any more? *(Someone shoves him on the crowded stairs.)*

4. Why does Brian find it strange that there are exactly fifty unsold boxes of chocolate? *(Usually there are a few boxes left unaccounted for.)* Why doesn't Brother Leon want to see the truth? *(All Brother Leon seems to care about is the result—the sale of all the chocolates—not how that result is obtained.)*

5. What does Brother Leon mean when he says that the law "one rotten apple spoils the barrel" has been disproved? *(Because of school spirit, the sale has been a success despite the fact that one student tried to ruin things by refusing to sell chocolates.)* Do you agree?

6. What happens to the fifty boxes of chocolate that Jerry hasn't sold? *(Archie has Obie set them aside to be raffled off.)*

7. How does the raffle work? *(For $1 each customer gets a chance at the candy and the $100 jackpot; the customer also writes one instruction for the boxing match—who hits whom and how.)* What fraction of the students do you suppose buy tickets? Would you buy one?

8. Why is Brother Leon the only adult who knows about the event at the athletic field? *(The event has been disguised as a football rally for students only.)*

9. How does Archie convince Jerry to agree to fight? *(Archie tells Jerry that this is a chance to get revenge on Emile.)* What do you imagine he has said to Emile to get him to agree?

10. At the boxing match, Archie feels that he has successfully conned Renault as well as the Vigils and the whole school. How has he conned Renault? *(He has gotten Jerry to "bring himself down" to Emile's level by engaging in violence.)* Do you think he has conned the others?

11. Emile and Jerry have both been double-crossed by Archie regarding the fight. How? *(Neither knows the terrible conditions of the fight until it is about to begin.)* Why doesn't Emile object? *(He thinks he can "handle" Jerry.)* Why doesn't Jerry object? *(He feels that he has come too far, has no other choice, has to strike back after all the harassment.)*

12. Why does Brian—who admires Jerry for standing up against the rest—agree to take charge of the lottery? *(Archie complimented his job on the chocolate sale and asked him to take over the lottery; Brian was "softened up" as well as intimidated.)* Where do you think the money which is not needed for the chocolate and the jackpot will go?

13. Why do you think Archie has admitted to Emile that there is no picture? *(Perhaps to further humiliate Emile, who sees what a fool he has been; also, Archie has gotten Emile to play right into his hands, so no longer needs to hold the photo over his head.)* How did Emile take that news? *(It made him angry, made him want to fight.)*

14. Do you agree with Archie that you can count on people to be two things: greedy and cruel (p. 175)?

15. What do Obie and Carter agree to do right before the fight? *(bring out the black box)* Why doesn't Archie simply refuse? *(The entire student body is watching and he would "lose face.")*

Prediction: How will the fight go? Will Jerry be glad that he "dared to disturb the universe"—or will he regret it?

Writing Idea
Rewrite the scene where Archie draws from the box of marbles. In your ending, everyone gets his "just desserts." (Good triumphs over evil.) Discuss in small group which ending is better.

Literary Analysis: Mood
The mood is the strongest feeling or emotion in a work of literature. Descriptions, conversations, and actions all contribute to the mood. What is the mood of this section? *(suspenseful, unhappy)* How is that mood built? *[descriptions of how Jerry is ignored, then harassed; Leon's chilling conversation with Cochran ("one rotten apple does not spoil the barrel"), Archie's ominous success in avoiding the black marble again]*

Chapters 37-39

Vocabulary

elemental 181   premeditated 182   catapulting 182

Discussion Questions

1. Why has The Goober been staying away from school? *(He is feeling depressed and physically ill from all that has been happening at school.)* Hasn't he been letting his friend Jerry down? Why do you think he goes to see the fight? Do you think there is an element of enjoyment in it for him, too?

2. What is "illegal" about the directions on one slip? *(They call for a dangerous, illegal blow to the groin.)* What is the result? *(Jerry tries instinctively to defend himself and the crowd thinks that he is showing cowardice; egged on by the crowd, Janza lets loose.)* Do you think the fight would have ended differently if the instructions had all been "legal"?

3. What is the "new sickness" that Jerry experiences when he lands a strong punch, catching Janza off guard (p. 183)? *(the knowledge that he is a beast like the others; He finds that he enjoys hurting Janza.)* Has Jerry allowed Archie to make him act like an animal?

4. Why do you think Janza is able to land so many blows (p. 184)? Is Jerry deliberately not fighting back? *(Jerry is stunned and may have given up in disgust with himself.)*

5. Why does the fight stop? *(Someone has told Brother Jacques, who turns out the stadium lights.)* Would Janza have killed Jerry?

6. How far does Brother Jacques go in confronting Brother Leon and Archie? *(Brother Jacques calls Archie the "villain" and asks why he did it, but when Brother Leon defends Archie, Brother Jacques voices only a mild rebuke: "I think we barely averted a disaster."—p. 188)* Why do you suppose he doesn't go farther? *(perhaps because he knows that Brother Leon is literally in control of the school right now)*

7. Do you think Brother Leon is as much to blame for what happened as Archie is? What consequences do you think each should suffer for what he has done?

8. What does Jerry try to tell the Goober? *(He tries to tell his friend not to buck the system, not to disturb the universe.)* Does he regret refusing to sell the chocolates—or just agreeing to the fight? *(He seems to regret refusing the chocolates in the first place.)* How do you think he will feel about the whole thing in a couple of days?

9. How do you feel as you read the end of the story?

10. How does Obie seem to feel about what has happened? *(Obie is pale as he agrees that they need to call a doctor; he seems shaken. He seems resentful when he tells Archie that maybe the black box will work the next time.)* How do you suppose Carter feels? Do you think this is the end of their efforts to cut Archie down a notch?

11. How does Brother Leon seem to feel about what has happened? *(He seems unconcerned about Jerry's injuries—simply satisfied that the chocolates have been sold and he is in control.)* What about Archie? *(He is very confident, pleased that he and Brother Leon are in control.)* How does Archie feel about Brother Leon at the end? *(Archie seems to be looking forward to further partnership with Brother Leon.)* Do you think Brother Leon has changed in his attitude toward Archie? Will "life at Trinity" go on as it always has?

Writing Idea
Follow Brother Leon home after the ambulance takes Jerry away. Describe his home and his actions as you imagine them. Try to shape your description so that it reveals what Brother Leon is like and how he is feeling about the outcome of the fight.

Literary Analysis: Theme
Point out that sometimes the author states one of his themes (central messages) directly by putting all or part of it in the "mouth" of the narrator. The title, repeated phrases, and the lessons learned by the characters are often clues to theme as well. For example, the title, *The Chocolate War,* emphasizes this theme: In everyday life, as in war, the distinctions between "good" and "evil" sometimes blur; as in war, anyone who risks challenging evil in today's world can be destroyed. The repeated references to Jerry's poster emphasize the centrality of that poster's message to the story: It is important to stand up for one's convictions, even if that means disturbing the status quo—and even if defeat is inevitable. The narrator makes explicit comments about these themes: those who are the victims of violence often end up feeling guilty; the "good" discover that they are capable of enjoying violence.

Post-reading Extension Activities

Post-reading Discussion Questions
1. What has Jerry learned from this whole experience?
2. Can you "relate" to this story? What makes it realistic—or unrealistic?
3. What is Cormier saying about the struggle between good and evil, in this story? Is evil victorious at the end? Is it hopeless to stand up for what is right? Or does the novel develop the idea that the individual must stand up for what he thinks is right—even if defeat is inevitable?
4. What questions do you have about this story?
5. What parts of this story might you change?
6. Does this story upset you?
7. Cormier's son, Peter, had his own experience with refusing to sell chocolates for a high school fund-raiser. How do you suppose he felt about having his experience made into a novel?
8. Throughout the novel, what were some examples of people conforming? of people standing up against the crowd? What does Cormier seem to be saying about conformity?
9. Of what other stories does this one remind you?

Suggested Further Reading
1. Other novels, stories, and essays by Cormier:

   Now and at the Hour (1960)
   A Little Raw on Monday Mornings (1963)
   Take Me Where the Good Times Are (1965)
   I Am the Cheese (1978)
   After the First Death (1979)
   Eight Plus One (1980)
   The Bumblebee Flies Anyway (1983)
   Beyond the Chocolate War (1985)
   Fade (1989)
   We All Fall Down (1991)
   I Have Words to Spend: Reflections of a Small-Town Editor (1991)
   Tunes for Bears to Dance To (1992)

2. Other books about pressure to conform and the "dark side" of human nature and group guilt are

   Lord of the Flies (William Golding)
   Animal Farm (George Orwell)
   Fahrenheit 451 (Ray Bradbury)
   That Was Then, This Is Now (S.E. Hinton)
   The Wave (Morton Rhue)
   I Know What You Did Last Summer (Lois Duncan)
   Killing Mr. Griffin (Lois Duncan)
   The Nicholas Factor (Walter Dean Myers)
   The Pigman (Paul Zindel)
   The Wild Children (Felice Holman)
   Bless the Beasts and Children (Glendon Swarthout)
   A Separate Peace (John Knowles)
   The Catcher in the Rye (J.D. Salinger)
   The Contender (Robert Lipsyte)

3. For comparison, view one of three films about mob behavior:
   - *The Wave* (about a classroom experiment on mob psychology that goes awry)
   - *The Children's Story* (a gripping film about the takeover of a country by a totalitarian government from the perspective of elementary students)
   - *Lord of the Flies* (about a group of British schoolboys who are stranded on a deserted island)

Writing

1. Alternate point of view: Retell a portion of the story (such as events leading up to Jerry's refusal to sell candy) from Jerry's point of view. Then tell the same portion of the story from Archie's point of view. Imitate the speaking style of each character as closely as you can.

2. Write a short "prequel" to the story which explains how Jerry ended up at Trinity.

3. Write the outline for a sequel to the story—then read and compare with the actual sequel, *Beyond the Chocolate War*.

4. Pretend that you are the writer of a video of *The Chocolate War*. You have decided to end the film with the fight scene. As Jerry and Janza fight, you will show Jerry's thoughts and memories in a series of rapid fire images that dissolve, one into the other. Write a description of all that the viewer will hear and see.

5. List and share all the writing possibilities that lie within and around the text. For example, Jerry might write a letter to an old friend about his new school, Archie might write a list of assignments, Jerry might write a "teacher poem," etc.

6. Compare this story with another story about conformity vs. individualism (e.g., *Lord of the Flies*). How are the protagonists' problems similar? Different? How is the theme of good vs. evil developed in both?

7. Write an acrostic poem about the novel based on its title.
8. Write a diamente poem showing how Jerry changes from the beginning of the novel to the end.
9. Recreate a copy of Archie's most recent report card, complete with any behavior problems he has.
10. Pretend that you are a new student at Trinity. Write a letter to someone at your old school, describing what has been going on at Trinity.
11. Write an epilogue which tells what has become of Jerry, Archie, and Leon twelve years later.
12. Write to the author with any questions/comments you have about the story.

Essay Topics *(See page 29 for an evaluation rubric for essays.)*
1. Compare how Cormier explores the theme of conformity vs. individualism in this book with how another novelist explores the same theme (e.g., Orwell in *Animal Farm* or Golding in *Lord of the Flies*).
2. Is Jerry finally free at the end of the novel? Support your answer with evidence from the book.
3. How is the power wielded by Leon and Archie like that exerted by particular real-life tyrants (e.g., Napoleon, Stalin, Hitler, etc.)?
4. Trace and analyze Christ/Holocaust imagery found throughout the book.
5. Is Archie evil?
6. Compare the two characters in the story who seem most like each other.
7. Contrast the two characters in the story who seem most different from each other.
8. Analyze how the novel explores the relationship of good and evil.
9. Analyze how the novel explores the abuse of power and authority.
10. Compare this novel with another by Cormier, such as *I Am the Cheese.*
11. Compare the growing terror in this novel with that in Arthur Miller's *The Crucible.*
12. Support the thesis that Jerry undergoes a moral breakdown at the end of the novel.
13. Support (or refute) this statement from the novel using evidence from your life or observations: "Funny, somebody does violence to you but you're the one who has to hide, as if you're the criminal" (p. 156).

Listening/Speaking
1. Find out all that you can about Robert Cormier. Then assume his persona and, with a partner, stage a mock interview.
2. You are a reporter for the *Trinity Gazette.* Write an article about this year's fund-raiser. Include interviews with Brother Leon, Archie, and other participants.

3. Create a taped "booktalk" in which you assume the persona of one of the characters in the story (probably Jerry, Archie, or Brother Leon). Tell just enough about yourself and one of your experiences to make listeners want to read the book.
4. Stage an "interview" with four students serving as a panel of characters (Jerry, Archie, Brother Leon, Emile Janza). Classmates pose questions (e.g., Jerry, why did you decide to keep refusing to sell chocolates? Emile, why did you agree to fight Jerry at the end? Brother Leon, don't you think the Vigils should be punished?) and students respond, remembering to stay "in character."

Debate

Stage a classroom debate about one of the following:
1. Most teenagers have a hard time going against the crowd.
2. Archie should undergo criminal prosecution for the attack on Jerry.
3. *The Chocolate War* does not belong in the classroom because it is depressing and contains obscenities.

(Those who agree get on one side of the room; those who disagree get on the other; those with no opinion stay in the middle. Both sides try to convince the undecided students left in the middle to join their side.)

Drama

1. Act out a particularly dramatic scene from the story, such as the scene where Jerry first lets Brother Leon know that he hasn't sold any chocolates.
2. Act out a scene we know about but never actually see, such as the conversation that leads to the group of boys going to help Goober unscrew the desks.
3. Act out a scene that doesn't happen in the story, but might have (e.g., What if Jerry had decided to try to talk with his father about some of the problems going on at school? What if Archie had given Obie an assignment?)
4. Imagine that you are the casting director for a made-for-TV movie based on *The Chocolate War*. Think of the two actors who would be your top choices for each part, and fill in a chart like the following:

Role	Physical Traits	Personality Traits	Two Top Candidates	Emotions He Needs to Portray
Jerry				
Archie				
Leon				
Goober				
Obie				

5. What if Brother Jacques had pressured other faculty to have a hearing about the final fight incident? Stage the "trial" of Brother Leon, Archie, and the Vigils.

© Novel Units, Inc. All rights reserved

Language Study
1. The author uses many examples of simile, metaphor, and personification. Make a list; include page citations. Discuss how these metaphors contribute to the theme and mood of the story.
2. Devise a vocabulary lesson based on the novel. What types of words play an important part in this book? If you were trying to teach six related vocabulary words, what would they be and why?

Art
1. Capture your impressions of Archie in any form you choose (paper maché sculpture, drawing, collage, etc.).
2. Create a poster that the Vigils might have put up to advertise the chocolate sale.
3. Create a five-frame "cartoon strip" that shows what happens in the scene that is most memorable to you.
4. Make a mobile or collage including some items that have importance in the story, such as a box of chocolates, a football, a box of marbles, or a paper making an "assignment." Use a coat hanger or half a paper plate, and attach the small items (which might be made of styrofoam or cardboard) with string.

Music
1. Choose music that sets the appropriate tone for a particular scene. Rewrite that scene as a radio play and record with the background music.
2. Create a jingle that the Vigils might have come up with to help sell chocolates.
3. Ballads are often about lovers, courageous heroes, tragedy. Choose the tune of a familiar ballad. Then write the words to a ballad about Jerry.
4. See if you can find a song that treats some of the themes found in the story (e.g., the abuse of power, the individual vs. the institution, etc.)

Research
1. Find out more about the psychology of group decision-making, conformity, and scapegoating. (You might start by learning about the famous research done in this area by Neil Miller and by Stanley Schacter.) What forces are at work on the boys at Trinity? How are these forces similar to those that helped create prejudice against Jews during Nazi times and against Blacks in the South during and after the Civil War?
2. Research an episode in history that parallels the tyranny of Archie (e.g., Why didn't more people rebel against Hitler? Are these the same reasons the students went along with Archie?)
3. Look up and discuss several samples of literary criticism written in response to this novel. Possible sources include: *Contemporary Authors, ALAN Review, VOYA, Horn Book*.
4. Create a bulletin board with newspaper and news magazine articles that touch somehow on the story (e.g., stories about real-life group intimidation, gang activity, etc.).

Evaluation: Rubric for Essay-Writing

The following is a suggested set of criteria for grading student essays. It can be altered in any way that fits the specific needs of a class. We encourage you to share the evaluation criteria with your students *before* they write their essays. You may even want to use this form as a self-grading or partner-grading exercise.

	Criterion	Maximum # Points
1.	**Focus:** Student writes a clear thesis and includes it in the opening paragraph.	10
2.	**Organization:** The final draft reflects the assigned outline; transition words are used to link ideas.	15
3.	**Support:** Sufficient details are cited to support the thesis; extraneous details are omitted.	15
4.	**Detail:** Each quote or reference is explained (as if the teacher had not read the book); ideas are not redundant.	15
5.	**Mechanics:** Spelling, capitalization, usage are correct.	15
6.	**Sentence structure:** The student avoids run-ons and fragments. There is an interesting variety of sentences.	10
7.	**Verbs:** All verbs are in the correct tense; sections in which plot is summarized are in the present tense.	10
8.	**Total effect of the essay:** Clarity, coherence, overall effectiveness.	10

TOTAL: _____

Comments:

ASSESSMENT FOR *THE CHOCOLATE WAR*

Assessment is an on-going process. The following ten items can be completed during the novel study. Once finished, the student and teacher will check the work. Points may be added to indicate the level of understanding.

Name _____ Date _____

Student   **Teacher**

_____   _____   1. Keep a response log as you read the book.

_____   _____   2. Discuss some of the book's themes before reading the book. Get prepared to enjoy and understand.

_____   _____   3. Keep a word list of new words you encounter as you read the book.

_____   _____   4. Make a list of literary terms for devices used in the book. Include a definition and example.

_____   _____   5. Collect your writing assignments done in response to the book. Choose two for revision, editing, and review.

_____   _____   6. Choose a post-reading discussion question from those on page 24.

_____   _____   7. Choose a writing or essay assignment from pages 25-26.

_____   _____   8. Choose a listening/speaking, debate, or drama activity.

_____   _____   9. Choose an art, music, or research activity.

_____   _____   10. Write a short critical review of the book in the manner of those in the Sunday newspaper.

Notes

Notes

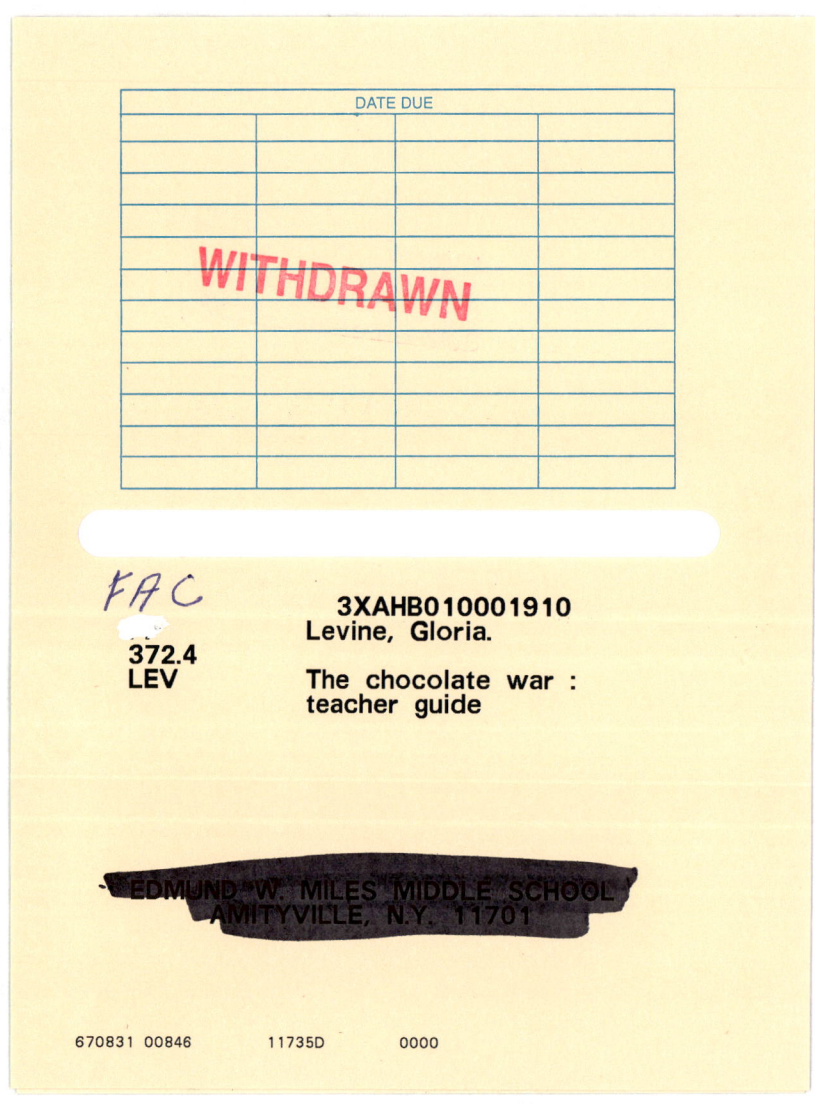